MY BIBLE STORY LIBRARY

MOSES
IN THE
BULRUSHES

Landoll, Inc.
Ashland, Ohio 44805
© Oyster Books Ltd. 1992

At one time long ago, thousands of Israelites called Egypt their home. But the Egyptians, forgetting how the Israelite Joseph had saved them from starving, began to complain.

"There are too many of these Israelites," they grumbled. "They will soon take over Egypt if we are not careful."

"If I put the Israelites to work," said the Pharaoh, "they will be too weak and tired to cause any trouble."

So cruel slave drivers forced the Israelites to make bricks and drag heavy blocks of stone to build cities and temples for the Pharaoh.

But still there seemed to be too many Israelites in Egypt. The Pharaoh decided to pass a very cruel law.

"All Israelite boys must be killed as soon as they are born," he announced.

Soon after this an Israelite woman, called Jochebed, had a baby son.

"I don't want them to kill my baby," she cried to her husband. "We must save him."

"We cannot hide a baby," her husband protested. "He will cry and the soldiers will find him."

But Jochebed had a plan. She made a cradle from rushes. She smeared the outside with tar to make it waterproof. Then she put her sleeping baby into the cradle and went down to the river Nile. She found a hiding place among the bulrushes which grew by the river bank, and left the cradle there, floating gently on the water.

"God will keep my baby son safe," she said to her daughter Miriam, who had come with her. "Stay here and watch what happens."

While Jochebed went home, Miriam too hid amongst the bulrushes and watched. Soon she heard the sound of laughter and chattering voices. One of the Pharaoh's daughters was walking

along the river bank with her servants. Suddenly, the Pharaoh's daughter noticed the cradle.

"Look!" she cried. "There is a cradle in the bulrushes. And there is a tiny baby inside."

One of the servants waded into the water and picked up the cradle. The baby, frightened by the sudden movement, began to cry.

"Poor little boy," said the Pharaoh's daughter, as she lifted the crying baby gently out of the cradle. "He must be an Israelite. I would like to keep him. I wish I knew someone who could look after him."

She spoke so kindly that Miriam felt brave enough to come out of her hiding place and speak to the princess.

"I know someone who could look after him," Miriam said. "I'll go and fetch her."

Miriam ran home and fetched her mother. They hurried back to the river.

"My name is Jochebed," said Miriam's mother. "My daughter tells me you have found a baby hidden in the bulrushes. I would be happy to look after him."

"Thank you," said the princess, not realizing that she was speaking to the baby's real mother. "I would like you to do that. Then, when he is old enough, I want you to bring him to the palace where he will be brought up as my son. I will call him Moses."

 Of course, Jochebed was overjoyed. Her clever plan had worked even better than she had hoped. No one would dare to kill her baby now that he was the son of one of the daughters of the Pharaoh.

Jochebed took Moses home and looked after him. The boy grew up strong and happy. When he was old enough to understand, Jochebed told him how God had saved him from death. She told him, too, that one day God would save the Israelites from their terrible slavery.

Finally the day came for Moses to go to the Pharaoh's palace. The princess was pleased with her fine young son, and thanked Jochebed for looking after him so well.

"Dress him in the richest clothes," she ordered. "I want him to be brought up like an Egyptian prince. He must have the best of everything."

Moses was given a splendid chariot and treated like a prince. Tutors came to the palace to teach him to read and write. But Moses never forgot that he was an Israelite. He never worshiped the strange, animal-headed gods of

the Egyptians. And every time he went out of the palace and saw Israelite slaves toiling in the blazing sun, he felt very sad.

"One day I will help my people," he thought.

As Moses got older, he became more and more angry with the way his people were treated. One day, when he was driving his chariot through the countryside, he saw an Egyptian beat an Israelite to death. Moses was so furious that he jumped down and killed the Egyptian. When he calmed down, Moses felt very ashamed of the terrible thing he had done. He looked around and, as no one seemed to have seen the murder, he buried the body in the sand.

The very next day, Moses went out and again was horrified to see two Israelites fighting each other.

"Stop!" he cried. "You should not fight. You are both Israelites."

"Who do you think you are to judge what we are doing?" asked one of the Israelites, rudely. "Are you going to kill us like you killed that Egyptian yesterday?"

Moses was terrified. Someone had seen what he had done. He knew that soon the story of his dreadful deed would reach the ears of the Pharaoh.

And that is exactly what happened. When the Pharaoh heard that Moses had killed an Egyptian, he was very angry. He wanted Moses put to death.

Moses knew that if he stayed in Egypt, he would be killed. So he fled at once to the barren country of Midian.

Before long he met a shepherd called Jethro. Moses became Jethro's friend. He went to live with Jethro's family and helped to look after their huge flock of sheep and goats. Eventually he married one of Jethro's daughters.

But Moses, although now a humble shepherd, had still more